GO WILD!

Frogs

Alicia Z. Klepeis

NATIONAL GEOGRAPHIC
WASHINGTON, D.C.

Hop ...

leap.

Jump,

splash!

Frogs can easily DART and DASH.

COMMON
WATER FROG

Let's explore the world of frogs.

All Kinds of Homes

AMERICAN BULLFROG

Frogs usually live in or near water. Some play in ponds or splash in swamps.

RED-EYED TREE FROG

COMMON WATER FROG

RIVER TOAD

Others make their homes in CREEPY caves, near WHOOSHING waterfalls, and on MIGHTY mountains.

They hop and hide in their habitats!

Around the World

Frogs live on all continents except Antarctica. It's too cold for frogs there!

Brazil has more kinds of frogs than any other country.

NORTH AMERICA
PICKEREL FROG

SOUTH AMERICA
AMAZON MILK FROG

AFRICA
PEACOCK TREE FROG

NORTH AMERICA

PACIFIC OCEAN

SOUTH AMERICA

ARCTIC OCEAN

EUROPE

ASIA

PACIFIC
OCEAN

AFRICA

ATLANTIC
OCEAN

INDIAN
OCEAN

**Frogs live in
the yellow areas.**

AUSTRALIA

SOUTHERN OCEAN

ANTARCTICA

EUROPE
PARSLEY FROG

ASIA
SPOTTED LITTER FROG

AUSTRALIA
HOLY CROSS FROG

Mighty and Mini

Big. Small. Short. Tall. So many sizes of frogs! The goliath frog is the world's biggest. Its body can grow to be longer than a ruler. And this heavyweight hopper can weigh as much as a newborn baby!

PAEDOPHRYNE
AMAUENSIS

The world's tiniest frog comes from Papua
New Guinea. This little leaper is the size of a
housefly. It weighs less than a popcorn kernel!

Look at Me!

Most frogs' bodies are designed for life on land and in the water. Take a look at the parts of this northern leopard frog.

SKIN: Frogs can breathe through their skin. They drink through their skin, too.

BACK LEGS: Long back legs help frogs jump far or zigzag away from predators.

TOES: Webbed toes help push frogs quickly through the water.

EARDRUMS: The circles behind a frog's eyes are its eardrums. They help the frog to hear.

EYES: Frogs can see really well in the dark.

TONGUE: A sticky tongue catches prey faster than you can blink.

VOCAL SAC: This balloon-like pouch of skin connects to a frog's mouth and makes its sounds louder. Only males have them.

NORTHERN LEOPARD FROG

HANDS AND FEET: Frogs have four fingers on their hands and five toes on their feet.

Enormous Eyes

Most frogs have BIG, BULGY eyes.
Big eyes help frogs find food and
escape from enemies.

They can even SEE COLORS IN
THE DARK! That's good, because most
frogs are active at night.

AUSTRALIAN GREEN
TREE FROG

15

Hide-and-Seek

Many frogs are brown and green, just like trees, leaves, and grasses. This camouflage is handy. It HELPS the frogs HIDE from predators and sneak up on prey.

VIETNAMESE
MOSSY FROG

Awesome Amphibians

Frogs are related to salamanders, newts, and caecilians. How are these animals alike? They are all amphibians.

Most amphibians spend some of their time in water and some on land. They are cold-blooded creatures that bask in the sun to warm up or slither into the shade to cool off.

YELLOW-STRIPED CAECILIAN

MEXICAN AXOLOTL

TIGER SALAMANDER

ENSATINA SALAMANDER

RED SALAMANDER

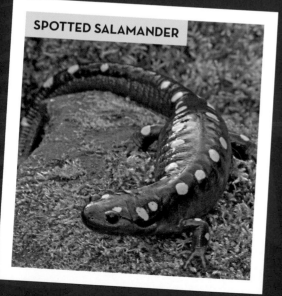

SPOTTED SALAMANDER

Nearly all amphibians have moist skin. Mucus helps keep their skin moist. This helps them breathe through their skin.

Tiny but Toxic

Unlike many frogs, poison frogs are active during the day. These jewel-like jumpers are bold and bright. The colors send a message to predators: "Stay away!"

STRAWBERRY POISON FROG

GOLDEN POISON FROG

HARLEQUIN POISON FROG

GOLFODULCEAN
POISON FROG

PHANTASMAL
POISON FROG

DYEING POISON
FROG

BLUE POISON
FROG

Most poison frogs are only as big as a paper clip. They come in a RAINBOW of colors and lots of pretty patterns.

On Their Own

Frogs are solitary animals. That means they mostly live on their own.

SPLENDID
LEAF FROG

COMMON
WATER FROG

But when they are looking for a mate,
hundreds of frogs might live together.

What's to Eat?

Spiders and slugs. Worms and bugs. Most adult frogs are carnivores. That means they are meat-eaters. Bigger frogs eat bigger foods. Mice, birds, snakes, and fish ... YUM!

ARGENTINE HORNED FROG

GREEN FROG

RED-EYED
TREE FROG

Frogs don't chew their food. Instead, they pull their bulgy eyes into the roof of their mouth. That pushes the food down into their throat.

DOWN,

DOWN,

GULP!

Sticky Spit

Most frogs hunt at night. They are fantastic food finders. Some hop about in search of a snack. Others are hidden hunters. They sit still and wait for prey to come ...

CLOSE ...

CLOSER ...

SNAP!

The frog's fast-flicking tongue flies out. Its spit is super sticky. No bug stands a chance.

GREEN TREE FROG

Baby Frogs

Many female frogs lay lots of jellylike eggs in water.

The egg mass JIGGLES and WRIGGLES. Then ... TA-DA! Tiny tadpoles hatch from the eggs.

As the tadpoles grow, an amazing change takes place. The tadpoles grow arms and legs. Their tails shrink until they are gone!

HOP! Now the tiny froglet LEAPS onto land.

29

Week 1:
Red-eyed tree frogs don't lay their eggs in water. Instead, they lay eggs on a leaf over water.

Week 2:
The tadpoles hatch and PLOP into the water below!

2–4 weeks:
The tadpoles begin to change. They grow arms and legs.

6 weeks:
Time to climb a tree!

1 month:
Now the tadpoles are froglets! The froglets move out of the water, but still have their tails (which they lose slowly).

2–3 years:
The froglets are now grown-up frogs! They are ready to have babies of their own.

5 years:
Red-eyed tree frogs in the wild can live to be five years old.

So Many Sounds!

Frogs make lots of noises to communicate. It's mostly males that make noises. They often call out messages to other frogs in the area. COME CLOSER! or GO AWAY!

Some calls you might know.

RIBBIT!

PEEP!

PINE BARRENS TREE FROG

JOHNSTONE'S WHISTLING FROG

QUACKING FROG

KO-KEE!

WHISTLE!

QUACK!

Others may surprise you.

Most frogs even SCREAM if threatened.

BUDGETT'S FROG

CROAK!

Frogs have lived on Earth for more than 200 million years. That's longer than many kinds of dinosaurs!

Frogs shed their skin regularly—and then (usually) eat it! Gulp!

A goliath frog can build ponds by moving heavy rocks.

WHITE-LINED LEAF FROG

In the winter, much of a wood frog's body can freeze. It's a frog-sicle! Don't worry, it thaws out in spring.

In some glass frogs, the heart can be seen beating through the transparent skin on the belly.

The southern cricket frog can jump more than 60 times its body length! That would be like an adult human jumping nearly to the top of the Washington Monument!

A frog can lift almost one and a half times its body weight with its tongue. That's like an adult human lifting a refrigerator with their tongue!

Frog Problems

Many frogs are in trouble today because of humans. People have cut down trees in rainforests where lots of frogs live. They have built homes and cities where the frogs' habitats were.

Disease is also a threat to frogs. A fungus attacks their skin. That makes it hard for the frogs to drink and breathe.

COMMON
WATER FROG

I  FROGS

Around the world, people are working to protect frogs. Frogs are an important part of the food web. They eat insects. They also provide food for animals such as snakes and birds. One way to protect frogs is by preserving places where they live.

AUSTRALIAN GREEN TREE FROG AT THE PERTH ZOO

TITICACA WATER
FROG

Lots of zoos, such as the Perth Zoo in
Australia, are helping frogs in another way.
They raise frogs born at the zoo and then
release some of the adults back into the wild.

How You Can Help

You can be a friend to frogs, too. Make a fantastic frog and toad abode!

RANID FROG

COMMON FROG

On the ground, place a flowerpot on its side. Prop it up with some rocks so frogs can hop in. If you have the space, ask an adult to help you create a pond where frogs can FROLIC and FEED.

An Eggs-cellent Game

Frogs aren't the only animals that start their lives in eggs.

Can you name these other animals that hatch from eggs?

1

2

Want to build your child's enthusiasm for frogs?

Visiting frogs at a zoo or animal park is a great place to start. Kids will be excited by their variety of colors, loud calls, and jumping abilities. Watching online videos is another terrific option, especially if there isn't a zoo with frogs near you. There are many amazing frog videos and articles on the National Geographic Kids website.

Here are some other activities for you and your child to do together.

Create a Rainforest Frog Habitat (Craft)

Materials: old magazines, construction paper, crayons and/or markers, scissors, and glue
Instructions: Help your child to find and cut out images of plants or other natural features (trees, waterfalls, etc.) they might see in the rainforest. Encourage them to glue these images onto the construction paper. After looking through the images of poison frogs or red-eyed tree frogs from this book, have them choose one to draw and color. When they are done, glue their colorful frog drawing onto the collage background.

So Many Sounds!
(Science)

Help your child discover the types of frogs that live in your area. Then research online what calls these frogs make. For example, the call of the western chorus frog sounds like running a finger over a comb's teeth. A cricket frog's call has a sound like quickly clicking two marbles together. Have your child try to mimic local frog calls with their voice or handy household objects. Take your child outside in the evening to see if they can identify any of the frog calls they've learned.

Can You Jump Like a Frog?
(Math and Movement)

Many frogs can jump more than 20 times their own body length. To help your child understand that distance, use a measuring tape to determine their height. You can mark their height on the ground with chalk. Multiply their height times 20. Then, from the same starting point, mark that distance on the ground. See how many jumps it takes your child to cover that distance.

Show-and-Tell!
(Public Speaking and Writing)

To celebrate World Frog Day (March 20), suggest your child bring a copy of this book to school, along with some pictures of different kinds of frogs from around the world and/or a toy frog, and share five fun frog facts. Take photos of their participation in the World Frog Day celebration and make a scrapbook together. It could include both your photos and the facts they shared with the class!

Spot the Spotted Frogs
(Research and Map Skills)

Many frogs around the globe have spots. The spotted grass frog (*Limnodynastes tasmaniensis*) lives in Australia. The crowned bullfrog (*Hoplobatrachus occipitalis*) lives in Africa. And the common frog (*Rana temporaria*) lives in Europe. Help your child research these three frogs to find out 1) if there are any similarities in the kinds of habitats where these frogs live, and 2) if their spotted patterns serve as any kind of camouflage in their native homes. Help your child print out a blank world map. Using one color per frog, have them color in the places in the world where each of these frogs can be found.

GLOSSARY

amphibians: a group of animals that includes frogs and their relatives

camouflage: the ability of an animal to blend in with its surroundings

carnivores: animals that eat only meat

continent: one of the seven main landmasses on Earth

froglet: a young frog in the stage between a tadpole and a full-grown adult frog

habitat: an animal's natural home

mucus: a thick, slimy substance that covers a frog's skin

poison: something that can hurt or kill living things if ingested

predators: animals that hunt and eat other animals for food

prey: animals that are hunted and eaten by other animals

solitary: animals that live on their own, not in groups

tadpole: the stage of a frog's life, typically spent in water, between an egg and a froglet

For Liliana, who loves going out to look for frogs and toads at night —A.K.

Cover, Thomas Marent/Minden Pictures; Back cover, Michiel de Wit/Shutterstock; 1, Mark Kostich/Getty Images; 2-3, KatarinaF/Shutterstock; 5, Paul van Hoof/Minden Pictures; 6 (UP LE), geraldmarella/Adobe Stock; 6 (LO RT), Lauren/Adobe Stock; 7 (UP LE), Albert Russ/Shutterstock; 7 (LO RT), mohd haniff abas/EyeEm/Adobe Stock; 8 (UP CTR), Gerry/Adobe Stock; 8 (LO LE), vaclav/Adobe Stock; 8 (LO RT), Intellifix/Alamy Stock Photo; 9 (UP), Wirestock/Adobe Stock; 9 (CTR), Daniel Heuclin/Nature Picture Library; 9 (LO), Bruce Thomson/Nature Picture Library; 10, Cyril Ruoso/Minden Pictures; 11, shandor_gor/Adobe Stock; 12-13, Riverwalker/Adobe Stock; 15, kuritafsheen/Adobe Stock; 16-17, Chris Mattison/Nature Picture Library; 18 (UP LE), Chien Lee/Minden Pictures; 18 (LO LE), cherokee4/Adobe Stock; 18 (LO RT), US Air Force Photo/Alamy Stock Photo; 19 (UP LE), Chris Mattison/Nature Picture Library; 19 (CTR RT), Mike Wilhelm/Adobe Stock; 19 (LO LE), John Cancalosi/Nature Picture Library; 20 (UP LE), salparadis/Adobe Stock; 20 (CTR RT), Thomas Marent/Minden Pictures; 20 (LO LE), Thomas Marent/Minden Pictures; 21 (UP LE), Alex Stemmers/Adobe Stock; 21 (UP RT), Mark Moffett/Minden Pictures; 21 (CTR LE), ZSSD/Minden Pictures; 21 (LO RT), mgkuijpers/Adobe Stock; 22, ondrejprosicky/Adobe Stock; 23, imageBROKER/Stefan Huwiler/Alamy Stock Photo; 24 (UP LE), Zaruba Ondrej/Shutterstock; 24 (LO), Christina Rollo/Alamy Stock Photo; 25, Chris Mattison/Nature Picture Library; 26-27, Brad Leue/Alamy Stock Photo; 28 (UP LE), Clara/Adobe Stock; 28 (LO), Ivan Kuzmin/Adobe Stock; 29 (UP RT), John Cancalosi/Alamy Stock Photo; 29 (LO), Richard A. Whittaker/Getty Images; 30 (LE), Bel/Alamy Stock Photo; 30 (CTR), Christian Ziegler/Minden Pictures; 30 (UP RT), Kike Calvo/Alamy Stock Photo; 30-31, All Canada Photos/Barrett & MacKay/Alamy Stock Photo; 31 (UP LE), Zigmund Leszczynski/Animals Animals/agefotostock; 31 (CTR), worldswildlifewonders/Shutterstock; 31 (UP RT), Dan Mihai/Getty Images; 32, Hamilton/Adobe Stock; 32-33, INTERFOTO/Alamy Stock Photo; 33 (CTR), pixelleo/Adobe Stock; 33 (UP RT), Geordie Torr/Alamy Stock Photo; 33 (LO RT), Milan/Adobe Stock; 34-35, Chien Lee/Minden Pictures; 36-37, Laurent Geslin/Nature Picture Library; 38, Cavan Images/Getty Images; 39, Pete Oxford/Nature Picture Library; 40, Thye-Wee Gn/Shutterstock; 41, Ashway/Alamy Stock Photo; 42 (LO LE), zhengzaishanchu/Adobe Stock; 42 (LO RT), fotoslaz/Adobe Stock; 43 (UP LE), fivespots/Adobe Stock; 43 (UP RT), Eric Isselee/Shutterstock; 43 (LO LE), Kraken Images/Adobe Stock; 43 (LO RT), Mirek Kijewski/Adobe Stock

Published by National Geographic Partners, LLC, Washington, DC 20036.

Designed by Kathryn Robbins

Library of Congress Cataloging-in-Publication Data
Names: Klepeis, Alicia, 1971- author. | National Geographic Kids (Firm), issuing body.
Title: Frogs / Alicia Klepeis.
Description: Washington, D.C. : National Geographic Kids, [2023] | Series: Go wild! | Audience: Ages 4-8 | Audience: Grades K-1
Identifiers: LCCN 2022023695 | ISBN 9781426373862 (hardcover) | ISBN 9781426375149 (library binding)
Subjects: LCSH: Frogs--Juvenile literature. | Frogs--Conservation--Juvenile literature.
Classification: LCC QL668.E2 K645 2023 | DDC 597.8/9--dc23/eng/20220615
LC record available at https://lccn.loc.gov/2022023695

The author and publisher wish to acknowledge the expert review of this book by Jodi Rowley, curator, Amphibian & Reptile Conservation Biology, Australian Museum & the University of NSW; Jeanne Robertson, associate professor of biology, California State University, Northridge; and the National Geographic book team: Shelby Lees, senior editor; Christina Sauer, associate editor; Colin Wheeler, photo editor; Alix Inchausti, senior production editor; and Gus Tello, designer.

Printed in China
23/PPS/1